11646949

Mother and Child

Mother and Child

by Jeanne Thwaites

South Brunswick and New York: A.S. Barnes and Company

London: Thomas Yoseloff Ltd

A. S. Barnes and Co., Inc.
Cranbury, New Jersey, 08512

Thomas Yoseloff Ltd
18 Charing Cross Road
London, W. C. 2, England

6501
Printed in the United States of America

For Josephine

Contents

A small section of the crowd on the wall waiting for the passing of the procession of elephants, the Kandy Perehera. In a span of 10 feet there are 15 people, 7 of which are children, and not a scowl among them. The Perehera is held yearly in August at the time of the full moon, and these people will have to come from all round the Island.

1

Mothers & Children of Ceylon

We were in Kandy, Ceylon. It was August, time of the Perehera — the great parade of the elephants which would bear the sacred relic, the Tooth of Gautama Buddha through the town. It was raining, but the crowds along the parade route had not thinned. Along the wall before us, perched high some 15 feet above the road, was a narrow parapet 1½ feet wide. This wall was crammed with people, mostly mothers and children, who had been waiting on the narrow ledge, six, seven, eight hours in the sun and intermittent rain. I counted 85 children in arms on the stretch of wall in my view. The little ones gazed happily around. They stretched out to tug at their mothers' hair, giggled when brothers and sisters beside them held up a friendly hand. But in the long wait in the open no child cried. Not one that I heard. No elder child provoked a younger to tears. No mother abused her little one. They sat together, animated, curious, smiling, a typical Ceylon crowd.

All over Ceylon I saw this same phenomenon. It could have been explained in a stoic race, but the Sinhalese are the most volatile of people. They are quick to laugh and to judge from the murder rate per capita — often the highest in the world — quick to anger. But their youngsters grow up in a warm climate where real hunger is rare among the village people. They have a strong sense of family and are hopelessly indulgent of their children. The children instead of reacting like spoiled brats, are sunny-natured and considerate of each other.

Religion plays a dominant part in the life of the people of Ceylon. Katragama shrine and river is a hive of hopeful pilgrims. People come to bathe in the sacred waters in the hope of miraculous cures. Or they may be carrying out a vow made for them by distraught relatives during illnesses from which they have recovered. Or they may bathe in the water to cleanse themselves of their earthly sins. Buddhists, Hindus, Moslems, all worship at Katragama. Mothers and children abound. Babies are anointed as are their parents with holy oils and ashes. This little one has been bathed in the river and anointed on the forehead.

On another section of the wall it was too narrow for sitting, but the children had begun to collect behind where the ground rose high enough for them to stand and sit and yet be able to see. For a moment a young woman and her child were silhouetted against the sky. The coconut trees are so much a part of Ceylon scenery that they have become a trademark of Ceylon pictures.

Only at Katragama would one see such a number of mothers and children gathered together. This particular group is like a child's puzzle "how many heads?" If you can spot the little one asleep on his mother's shoulder, you should come up with eleven.

The Sinhalese, and the Tamils who also populate Ceylon and originally came from South India, are both goodlooking races. The children have enormous black eyes and jet black hair. Their skins are brown and silky. They are often really beautiful. The little girls are modest, shy, and utterly feminine. The boys playful, energetic, but also unexpectedly shy when faced with a camera. When they are fortified by numbers, they come round to stare curiously at a stranger. But when the camera turns on them they hide their faces.

"And an effort to do it herself."

The Tamils are the second race who live in Ceylon. The arrogant young woman with her little daughter is Tamil. Young Tamil girls mature early and are at their most beautiful in their teens. They are much more aggressive than the Sinhalese girls of the same age, openly flirtatious and are lively and full of fun. This young woman was among the pilgrims at Katragama and as she is a Tamil she would be a Hindu — not a Buddhist.

14

There is no one who feels more strongly about a very tiny baby than a mother whose own infant has started growing up. Perhaps this is what keeps the population of the world growing! The woman on the left triggers some of my own emotion when I see a new baby. I wish it were mine.

The Tamils and Sinhalese are of completely different race and they speak different languages which even have different scripts. This woman is Tamil and one can tell her race even by the jewelry she wears: the distinctive earrings and nose-studs. The nose-studs are fastened from the inside of the nostril just as an earring is fastened through a pierced ear. The Tamil has a wider face, wider cheekbones, broader nose, thicker lips, and invariably has curly hair. The complexion is darker than the Sinhalese. They have a reputation for being both industrious and honest and are much in demand as workers.

Another Tamil woman at Katragama. It is not often one sees women nursing their babies in public in Ceylon but this one is handling the task without embarrassment to anyone. The crowds and heat at the shrine exhaust everyone and towards the end of the day faces show the strain.

Here in Katragama people hope to find the cures for their troubles and illnesses. The mother in this picture has lost one eye but her face suggests even greater tragedy and her baby looks ill. They disturb my peace of mind.

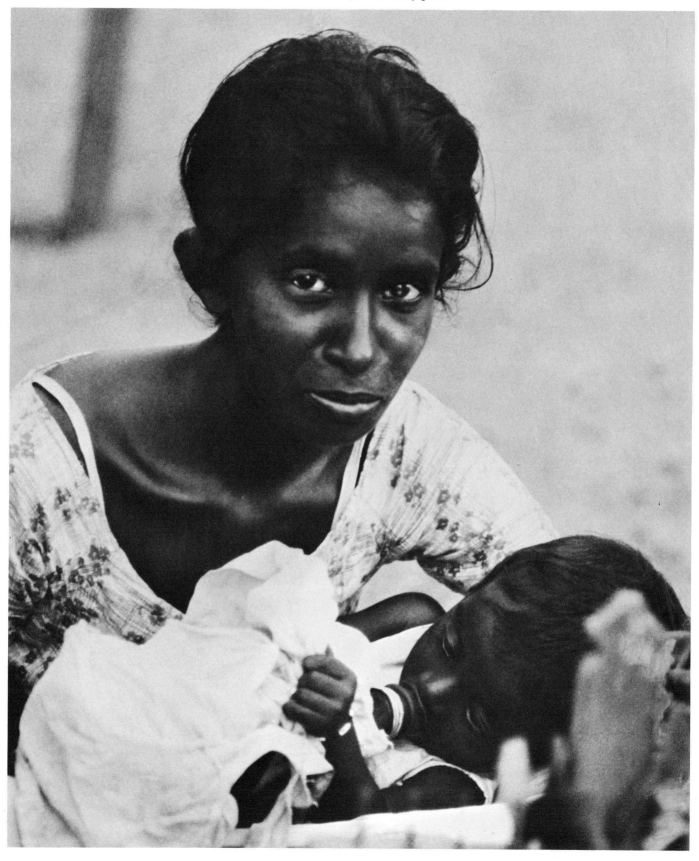

Through the crowd we glimpsed mothers trying to cope with children and here is one such moment.

Another tired face. Again and again we saw such tired women and such contented babies.

The age-old way of solving the problem of how to cope with tired legs and a tired little girl. But we are all so civilized now that our backs would give way if we tried it for long! And the little figure on the right — boy or girl?

This woman dressed in her best sari would be coming to give thanks at the Shrine.
The white marks on the foreheads of the crowd are holy ashes. A hand stretches
out to touch the infant and the mother beams with pride.

Another mother, very young and with a very beautiful baby.

North of Ceylon is Jaffna, populated by Tamils who migrated from South India. Colombo has temperature of about 80°F. throughout the year. Jaffna is not only hotter but drier. The Tamils from there are called, appropriately enough, Jaffna Tamils! This is to separate them from the Tamils from South India. Tamils are no longer allowed to work in Ceylon, except in certain special capacities, unless they were born on the Island. This poses no problem among Jaffna Tamils whose families have lived there for generations. This picture was taken at the Hindu temple in Jaffna during the festival. All manner of penances were carried out, the most spectacular being the rolling around the temple. The poor sinners (men, of course) undress to loin cloths and lie down in the sand outside the temple. Then they roll themselves all the way around the actual building. As they roll they get sweaty and the sand sticks to them and they get hotter and dirtier. This gets rid of their sins. They should roll continuously but it is exhausting work and all have to rest every few minutes. Tempers inside the temple become short with the heat and the crowds. For the first time in Ceylon I saw children crying lustily and mothers snapping at them. While I watched this youngster weeping, the woman who was talking with a friend leant over and slapped him across the face as her blurred hand shows. When she saw I had captured the moment for posterity she rolled about laughing and so did everyone else!

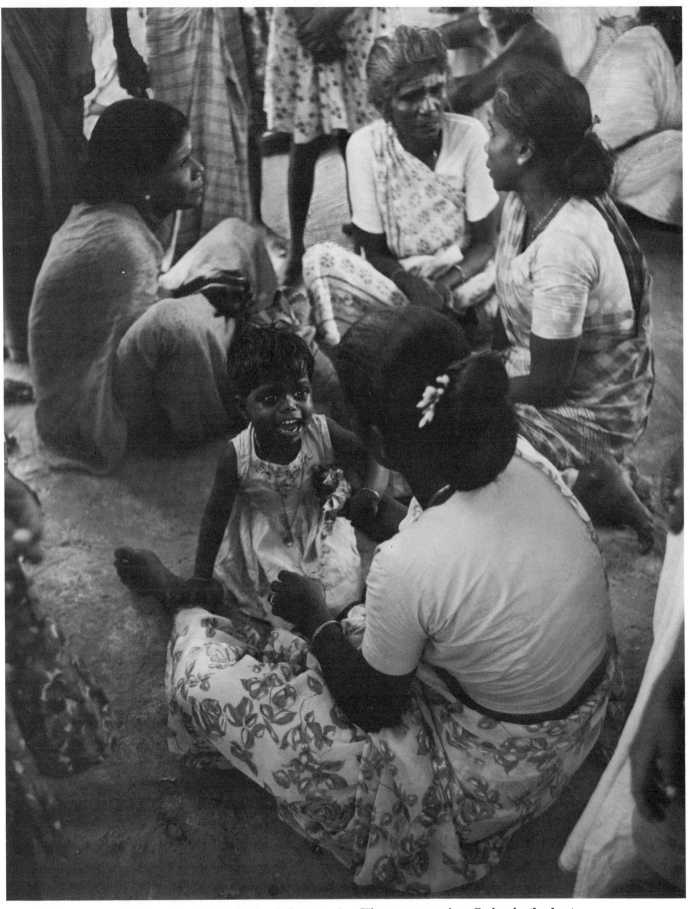

Another Tamil baby in the Jaffna temple. His temper too is suffering in the heat.

They look one straight in the eyes. Their smiles are therefore the more infectious, their glance bridges difference in age, race, and upbringing thus conveying a feeling of immediate rapport with each individual they meet. This habit of looking straight at one struck me as being unusual as the adults do it too. Many Oriental races do not look at one at all, it seems, and certainly the Western and so-called civilized races have forgotten what it is to look at every single person one passes as an individual. But the overall feeling it gives is that they care. They notice you and care about you.

The grace of the Ceylon women when handling their children gives them a Madonna-like beauty. They are openly tender with their youngsters. They delight in showing them off. And they pass these characteristics to their daughters so that even the smallest little girl has the same gentle loving patient qualities when handling babies.

There is an expression in Sinhalese which literally translated means "to just be." This is often used in the context of "to stop moving around needlessly," "to stop agitating," etc. These people have mastered the art of "just being." Tranquility in movement and an ability to stand or sit absolutely still are their distinctive characteristics.

The mothers and children of Ceylon personify all these qualities — patience, a good nature, beauty, curiosity, kindness, rapport and the ability to "Just be."

Any woman who has been pregnant has to feel for this weary young girl in the later stages. She has even stuck a pacifier in the mouth of her little girl to quiet her. This woman is wearing a long dress, which is a village garment worn wherever the Catholic missionary influence has been strong. Like all Ceylon women she makes no effort to hide her pregnancy and looks much more graceful as a result.

On the country roads one sees the grace of Ceylon women. This is a very typical Sinhalese with her toddler. The "jacket" and "cloth" is the native costume of the Sinhalese. The sari is not worn except, in certain areas on special occasions, by the Tamils, or by the rich. The drape of the cloth and the style of the jacket varies slightly from province to province. Nowadays small girls invariably wear dresses, though one sees a lot of young boys who wear "sarongs." This is not the same garment as the women's "cloth" which is a strip of material wrapped around the waist. The "sarong" is a tube of material which the men and boys climb into and then twist around themselves to fit tight and secure with a belt.

27

These two women are Tamil. They wear sari and not the cloth and jacket, or the long dress of Sinhalese village women.

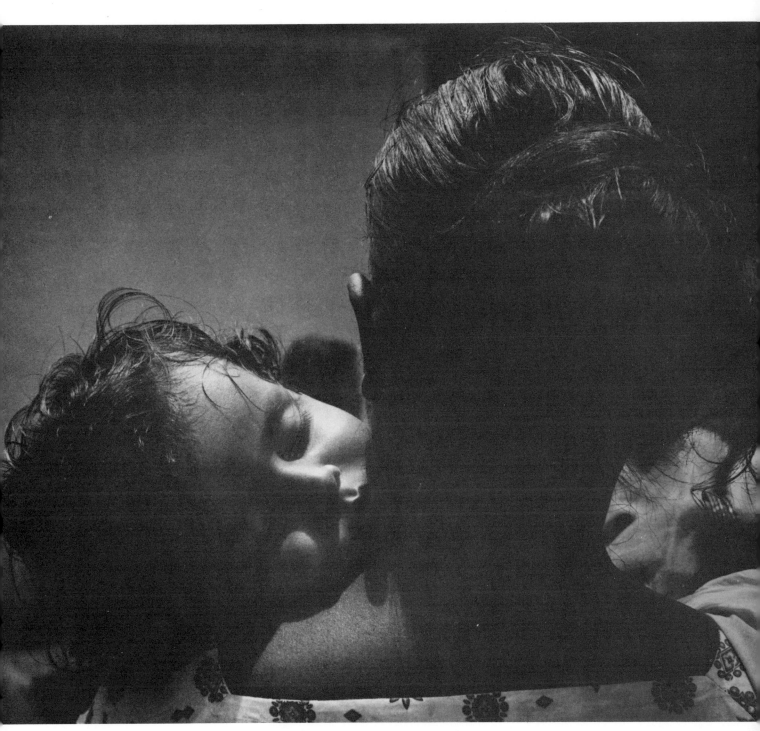

A weary infant at the end of a long day.

The beggar women of Colombo are notorious. Rich women who are accosted by them as they hold out their tin begging cups to cars which have to slow down or park in front of shops, write letters to the papers indignantly decrying them as a "disgrace" to the country. If the beggar women have no young babies of their own, they rent them from mothers who are extremely poor. Many good-looking beggar women are prostitutes by night and beggars by day, and the authorities have a fine time trying to channel them into more worthwhile occupations! But the women have cheerful smiles and are unconcerned with their sinful ways.

Father, mother, baby.

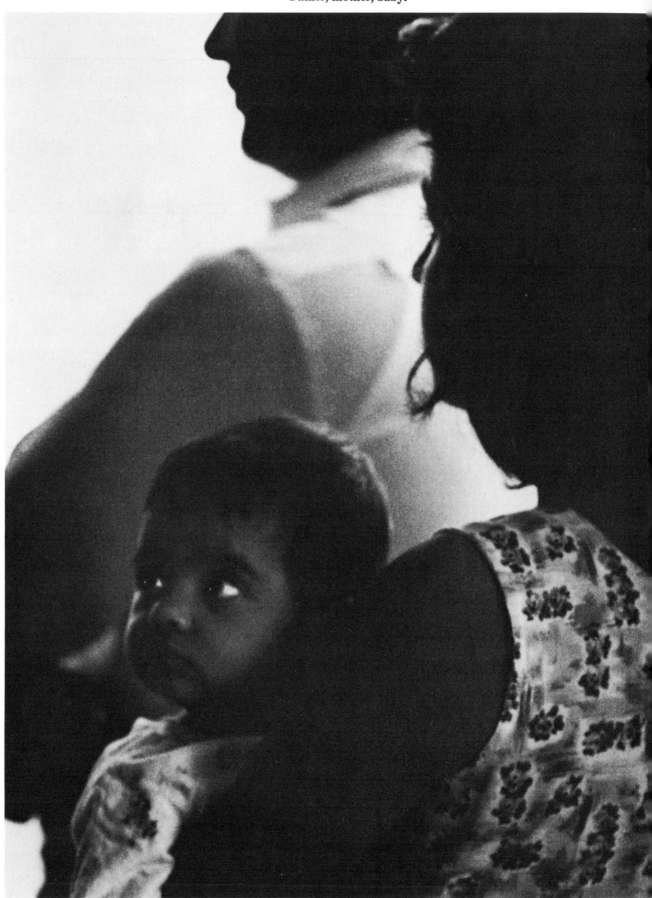

In the dark recesses of a shop I saw this woman with her child.

A very beautiful Sinhalese girl with her little boy.

A tender moment between mother and child.

2

Water Babies

The National passion of the Sinhalese is bathing. They are a fastidiously clean people and as an Island race love water. Ceylon's climate is tropical and generally water is plentiful. But even in the Dry Zone where it is not, the Sinhalese make an effort to get down to a river, or to find a tap where they can bathe every day. This has nothing to do with their economic circumstances. To rich and poor the daily bath is an absolute minimum of washing and personal cleanliness is almost a fad. A young European girl, who took pride in her own high standard of cleanliness, married a Sinhalese. She was stunned to find that her husband changed his shirt 40 times each week! When the Sinhalese bathe, this means they wash their hair too. In fact they make it a point to refer to a "body bath" if that is all they are going to wash! Throughout Ceylon one notices that however poor a family may be, they, and their clothing, are shiningly clean. The Ceylon villages are therefore a real pleasure to walk through. Even the terrible smell one usually associates with Eastern villages is missing.

Families bathe at the river together. No one, except the children, strips for the bath. The woman moves the "cloth" she normally wears tied at the waist and re-wraps it under her armpits. She can then remove all her clothing from under it and wash and soap herself under it too. Men wear shorts or loin cloths. The whole business of taking a bath is as much pleasure as an effort to keep clean.

37

Bath time is a good time to wash clothes.

This family has found a field under water and in they go.

Bathing by moonlight.

Two boys each see to it that the other gets clean — and they use as much energy as possible for the task.

On a lonely upcountry road I came across this beautiful young mother bathing her little girl in a basin of water. Condensed milk cans or powdered milk cans, such as she is using for a cup, appear in many pictures. Canned goods are not within the price range of most people but in a country where milk is not plentiful, canned milk has to be used when it is needed. Milk cans are used as bathing cups, household containers, drinking cups, beggar bowls, and for a variety of other uses.

Often one will find someone bathing under the village faucet, which is the source of water for the entire village. Household water is carried by the women and these contented rural people make the business of fetching water a happy social occasion. Here is one family filling up for the day.

The clay "chatties" in which water is carried give an added grace to the women who carry them. These three women came swinging easily down the road but their chatties of water must have been very heavy. The little girl carries something more to her size — a condensed milk can.

44

Two women paused a moment to rest on the road. This was no pose, they stand this way instinctively.

A pretty girl with her chatty on her head and an appreciative eye from a passerby.

A fountain of water means just one thing to the Sinhalese, it is somewhere to wash.
This is in Kandy.

The tiny babies at Nayakakanda stay in an annex which is called the Creche. Here their mothers may stay with them, but sadly, few take advantage of this. Most women return to their villages leaving their infants with the nuns. This Sister is in charge of the Creche. She sadly notices that no baby, however carefully tended by the Sisters and older girls from the school, does as well as under a single mother's care. She says "we are often kinder to them than their actual mothers, but they need a single mother's love." The children call the nuns "Mother" and everyone else calls them "Sister" — because "we are Mothers to the children and Sisters to each other."

3

Some Unusual Mothers & Children

Buddhism and Hinduism are not the only major religions of Ceylon. There is a surprisingly large Catholic Section. It is quite easy to see Catholic missionary influence. The women in villages wear long dresses rather than the traditional jacket and cloth. They wear medals around their necks, carry rosaries and have holy pictures in their homes.

The Good Shepherd order of Nuns are among the most active workers with the poor. They have a number of Convents in the Island. One of their projects is at Nayakakanda where they have a large orphanage. Anyone who may have suspected that nuns are frustrated creatures who give up the responsibilities of the world for a life of seclusion should visit this orphanage. The nuns not only lavish these children with love and care, but they try in every way they can to fit them for a useful life in the world. When the children are adopted the Sisters keep an eye on them for many months before satisfying themselves that they are getting more love, more security, in fact that they are getting a better deal all around than they would under the care of the nuns themselves.

The children come to the Convent not only because they have lost both parents. Their parents may not be able to keep them for a variety of reasons — they may be in jail, and of course many children are merely illegitimate. In such cases the nuns try to enable the mothers to stay with their babies by providing a cottage industry in the actual convent grounds — a handloom weaving center where the mothers can work for wages and support themselves and their babies.

The pre-school children are taught by the Montessori method, the very same method taught at the Good Shepherd convent in Colombo which is attended by some of the richest children in Ceylon. The entire organization of these and the other Good Shepherd projects in Ceylon is by a most enlightened nun, Mother of Good Counsel, Mother Provincial of the Order in the Island. Like a female Pope John she has a gift for sweeping cobwebs out of everyone's heads and really getting things going without fuss or misunderstandings.

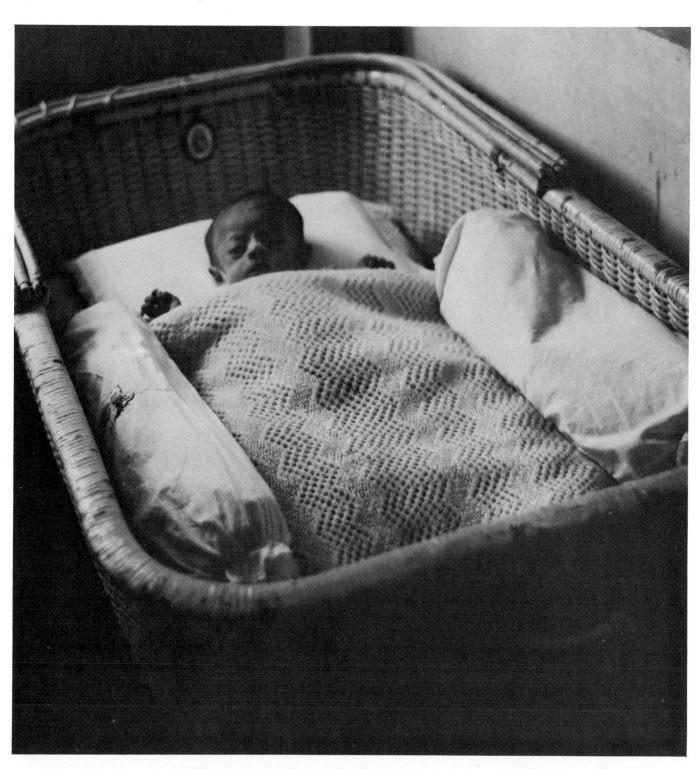

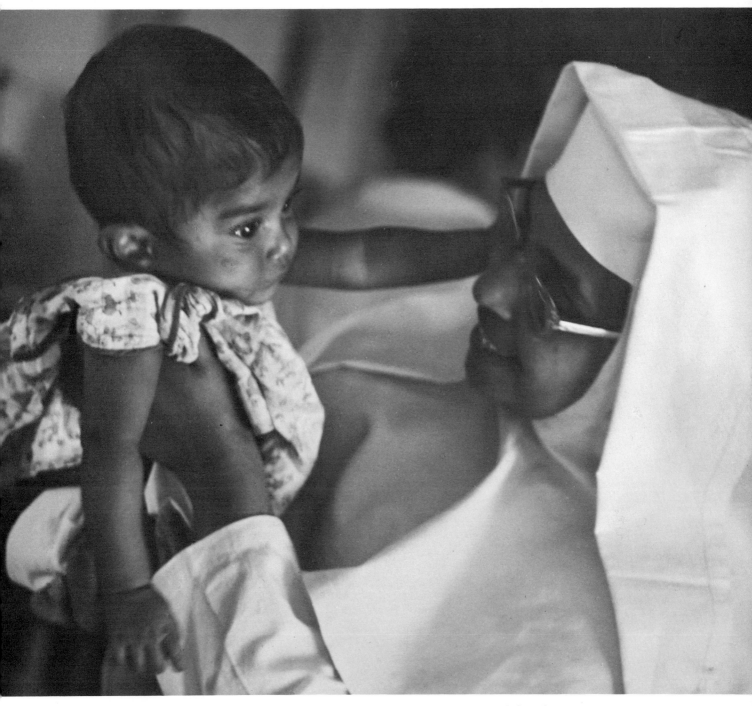

This is another sister who runs the Creche. She picked up this infant for a hug because at that moment everyone was fussing over the baby in the next crib.

This is no newborn infant but a little boy several months old. A few days later he took a turn for the worse and died. His mother was an unmarried crippled girl. Although she had intended to keep her baby she suddenly changed her mind. He was a healthy baby but contracted two illnesses before he was two months old. Then when he appeared to be out of the woods he became ill again. The Sisters put him in this special basket and as if willing him to live said "look at him, just like a little prince." But he was too weak to survive.

51

In the Montessori schoolroom the Sisters encourage the children to do everything
themselves. When the children take something out they put it back when they are
finished and this becomes second nature to them. When they do something new
they are taught the correct way the first time. But all this is done very gently and
persistently and they enjoy themselves thoroughly. This Sister is helping a new-
comer to the class. She patiently tries to get him to move the table he had just
pushed out back where it belonged. The little girl on the left is an old hand at
this sort of thing.

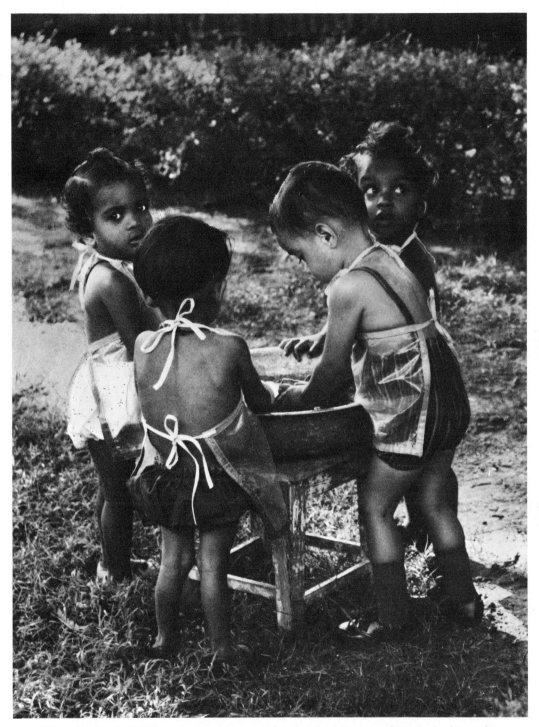

The preschool children are taught everything by the Montessori method of learning. These four toddlers are learning to wash. First you wet the hands, then you apply the soap, then you put the soap back . . . and very soon they can do it without prompting.

The children work with great independence. No prompting made this boy water the plants but he went about the task with great care.

One of the little girls dropped something on the floor and immediately got the broom and swept it up. When she was through she put the broom back. All this was unprompted.

As the children get to the age of six the boys leave the orphanage for a boys' school. The girls stay at the Convent unless they are adopted. They grow up and go out into the world, but unless they marry they consider the Convent their home. They are in great demand as working girls because they are excellent seamstresses, adept at all household tasks and have handled small children since the time they were children themselves. This little group has just come in from prayers in the chapel.

This is Tarala, one of the new projects of the Good Shepherd Nuns. It is a small village without any industry to keep its people busy. The Sisters hope to start another weaving center. The Sisters never pass a child without stopping, and the children are not one bit shy of the nuns but rush out of their homes when they hear they are visiting.

4

Girls

The Sinhalese girl is a very gentle creature, shy and unwilling to be photographed. The Sinhalese race is Aryan. This is extremely unusual in a brown-skinned race. One can see the Aryan features in these little girls' faces by imagining a fair skin, light hair, blue eyes. The faces themselves have the same construction as little girls born to any Northern country.

This is a typical little Sinhalese girl.

Three little girls wandering around the market place together. They each wear a different style dress. This was in an East Coast town.

Here is the tallest of the three closer up. A real Tamil beauty . . .

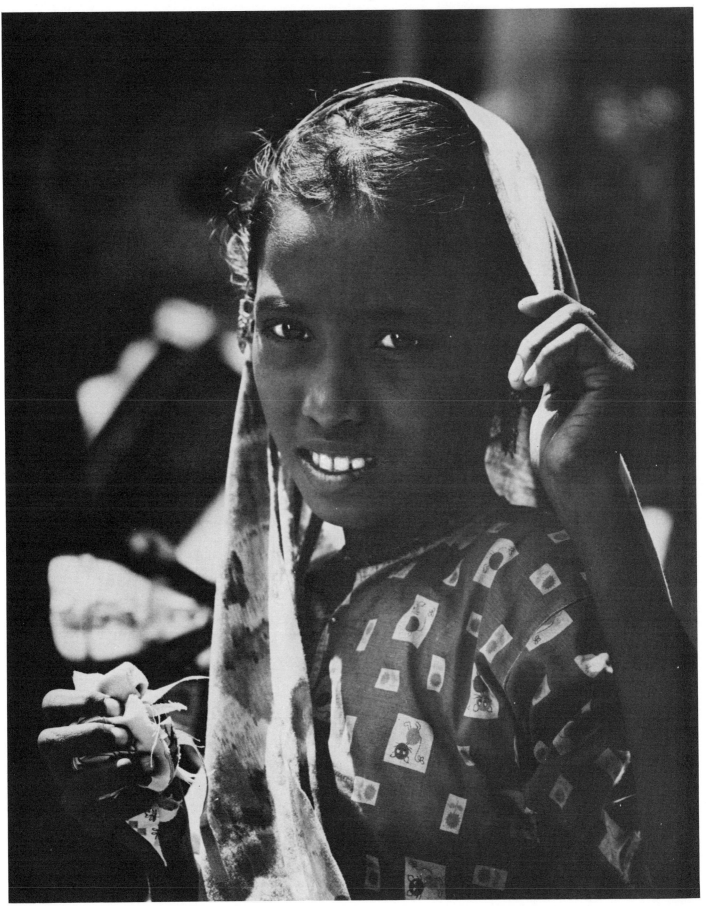

The middle one, who looks something of a tomboy . . .

The littlest one.

Another lovely girl was waiting to go into the temple carrying her sticks of incense.

The betelnut seller. The Sinhalese chew betelnut even though it discolors their teeth. The paste which she is putting in the leaves is in a milk can.

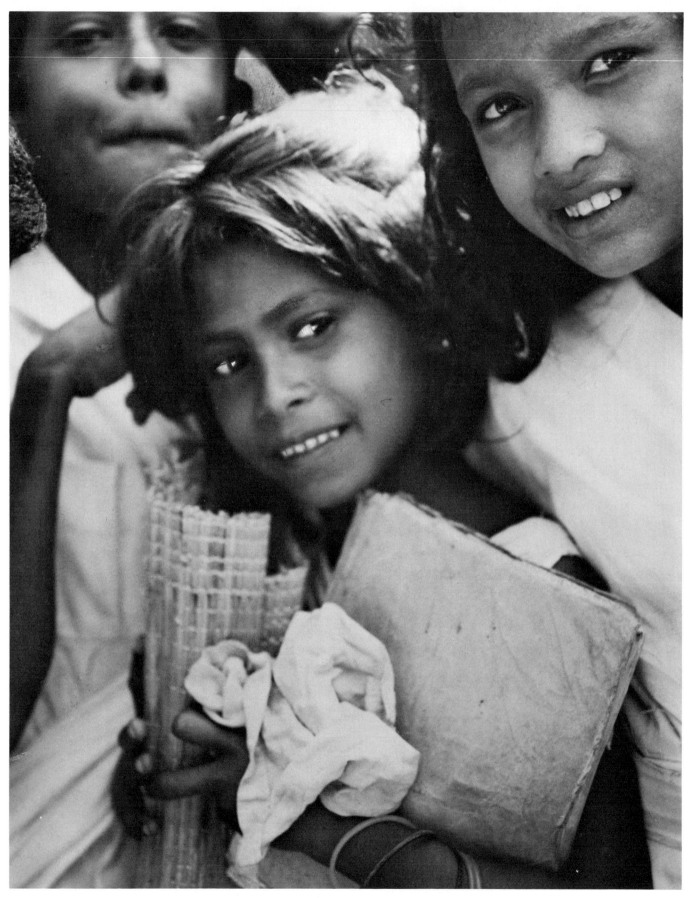

This little girl stopped at the temple on her way home from school.

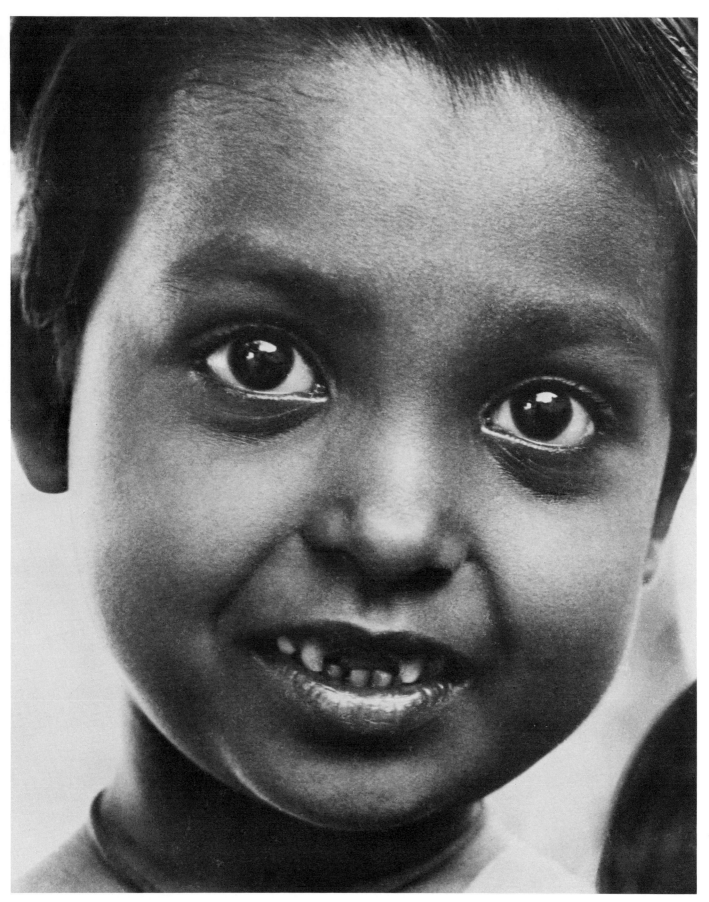

Six years old.

It is unusual to find saris worn by young
children. These are Tamil girls.

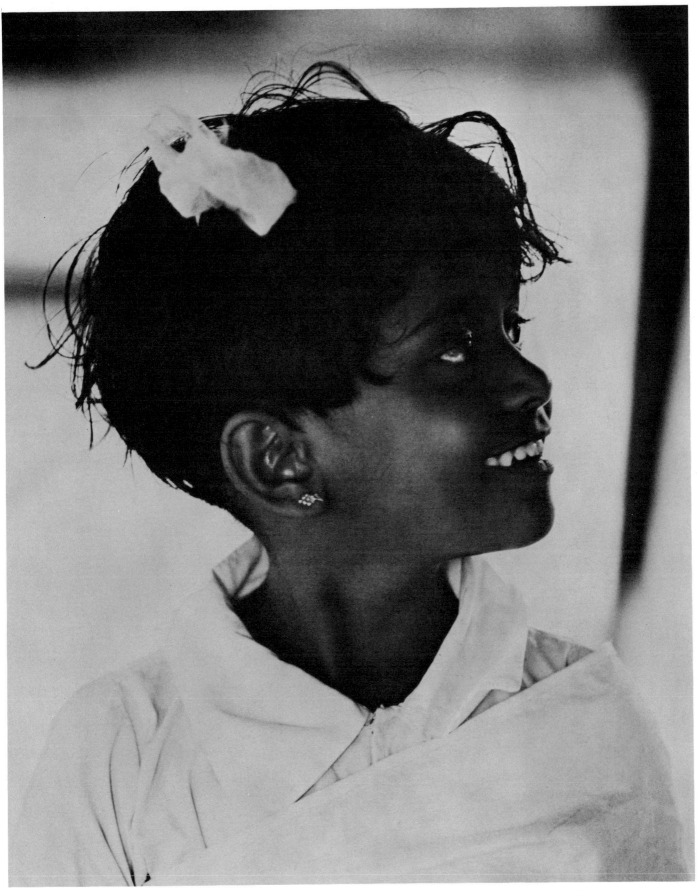

One gets the feeling that her smile has something to do with the ribbon in her hair.

The roofs of most huts are thatched and made from the coconut palm leaves. This is done by hand. Although this young girl is poor, her petticoat is edged with handmade lace.

The most distinctive feature of Sinhalese children is their enormous black eyes.

Little girls from a market place.

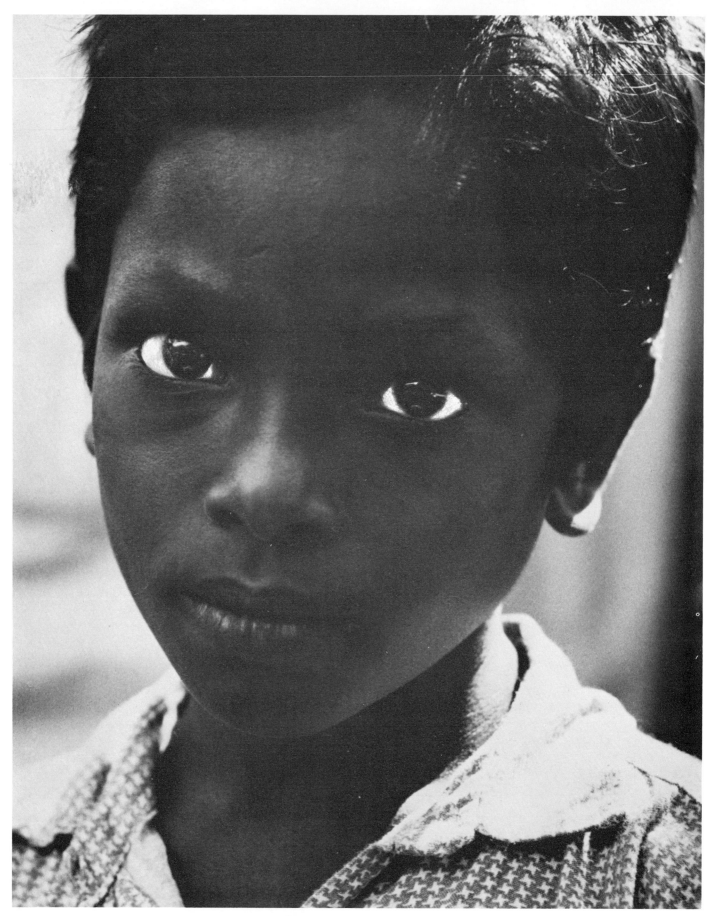

This boy has classical Sinhalese good looks.

5

Boys

Each boy is looking straight at you. The fearless inquisitive look is to me their most distinctive feature, even more than the obvious beauty of some of the faces. When the Sinhalese boy grows up he often keeps much of this beauty and it is a little disconcerting to find tough men in all walks of life who still gaze limpidly from enormous lustrous eyes and half-inch long eyelashes.

The boys help their fathers as the girls help their mothers. In Negombo, fishing is the occupation of the people and here is one youngster taking the nets out to his father's boat.

In contrast, two little devils with nothing better to do than fool around in the market place.

77

A four-year-old.

Two faces in a crowd of school boys.

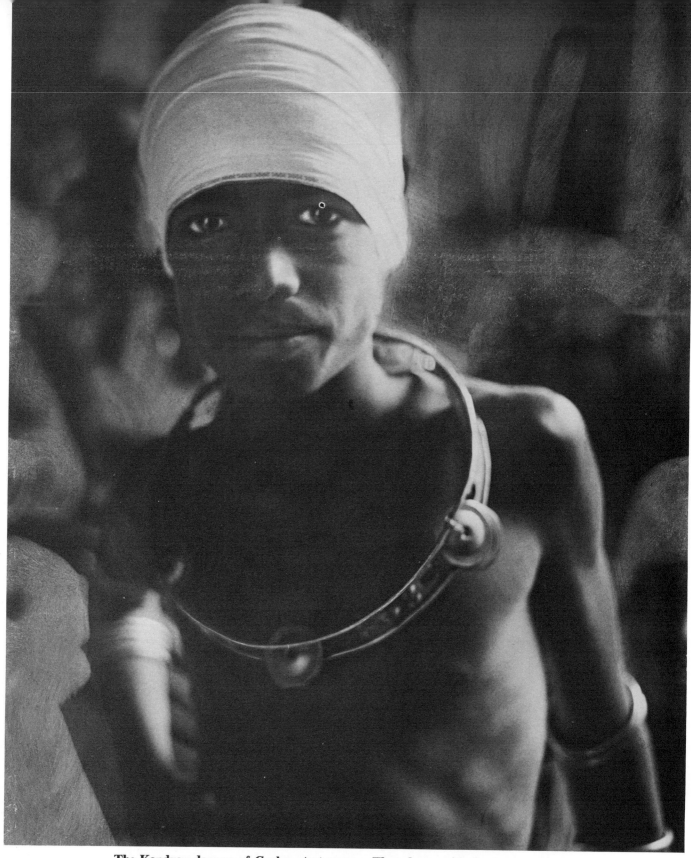

The Kandyan dancers of Ceylon start young. They dance with the troupe as soon as they are competent and graduate as qualified dancers when they are considered sufficiently proficient by the older experienced dancers. This boy will dance in the Kandy Perehera and help the "rhythm section" with his tambourine.

This youngster, on the other hand, is a full-fledged graduate dancer as his hat and costume show. He too is preparing for the Perehera, but even while dressing he shows grace and polish in every movement.

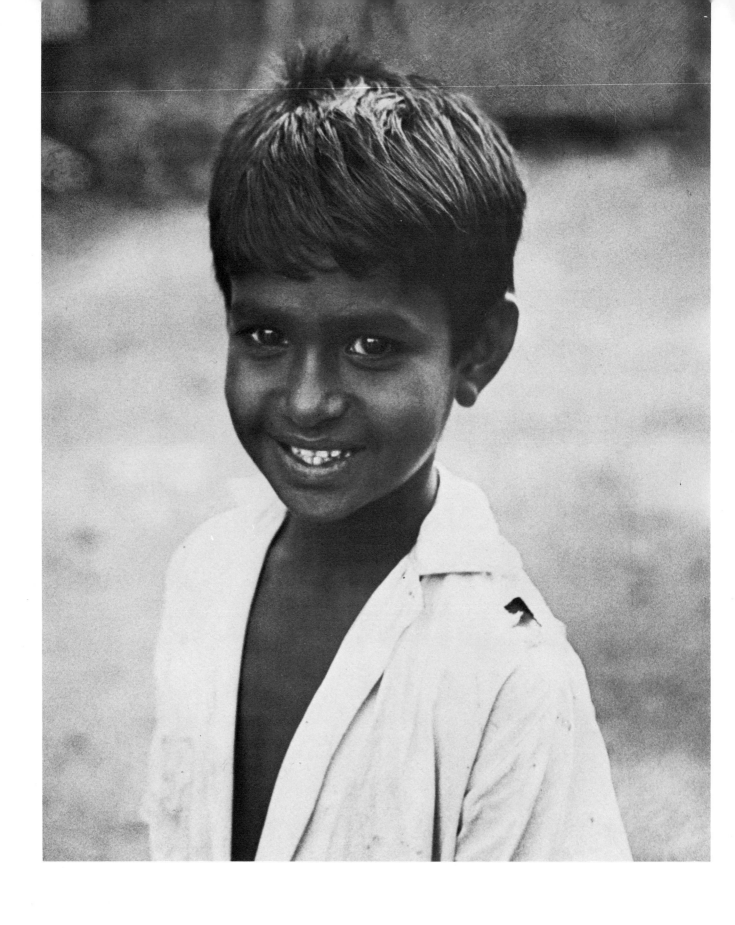

Two goodlooking young men from the market place.

A boy? Yes, really.

Once in a while in a crowd of children one comes across one child with "star quality." Just a fisher boy from Negombo but a young man who could go anywhere on charm, poise, and looks. While I was wondering how to photograph him without making him self-conscious, he saw the camera turn towards him, looked straight at it and smiled this marvelous smile. A born actor.

6

Two Chinese Mothers

Ceylon women carry their babies in their arms. En route to Ceylon, passing through Hongkong, I took a couple of pictures of Chinese women and their babies. In both shots one sees how the convenience of the piggy-back ride frees the arms of the mother.

7

Ceylon Exteriors

The Dutch Interiors are distinctive because of the still-life quality of the figures in them. They are, in fact, still life paintings. The figures are merely human beings used instead of vases, etc. Or so it seems to me.

We were in a Ceylon village off the main road and there were no roads for cars. It had once prospered but the richer people had moved away and the houses were a little more substantial than is usual in small Ceylon villages. But the nucleus of the village remained.

The people came out to see us. As they stood around talking to each other or merely staring, a still-life quality in them struck me very forcibly. These people instinctively arrange themselves in decorative groupings and I was reminded of the Dutch Interior paintings.

A family group. The house is beginning to crumble and there is another baby on the way, but this family is as happy as can be.

No sooner had this mother realized that I was going to photograph her child than she was pulling a dress over her head. When she saw she was too late, she took it right off again!

You can see clearly the still-life quality of this arrangement. I love the little boy so neatly covered above so inadequately below!

Another grouping that is all movement, yet the three figures in front have a composition that would be graceful if they were objects rather than people.

Here are some of the problems I would expect when photographing a mother and her four children:

The children will fight, cry, push, want a drink of water —

The arrangement will probably look contrived, stiff, like a criminal line up —

At least one child in each final shot will look like hell. Yet one shot of this little family and voila!

This is the street between two houses.

94

In Ceylon the older generation are not pushed off into groups of other old people but play an important function in the family life. They are treated with respect and nursed when they get old. They cook for the family, boss the younger people around, and it is all considered a part of life. Grandma here had the longest tooth I ever saw, and apparently it was the only one she had.

8

Childhood

Children throughout the world have one thing in common: gestures. They bridge all barriers. They are brainwashed out of us by our parents and teachers because what is normal behavior in a child becomes socially unacceptable in a grownup. But when we see these universal gestures and expressions of children we have to smile because they trigger the nostalgia in us.

Here are some of childhood's spontaneous reactions.

There will always be a thumbsucker . . .

Or a finger sucker . . .

Or a hand sucker.

There are those children who stick their tongues out and here are two.

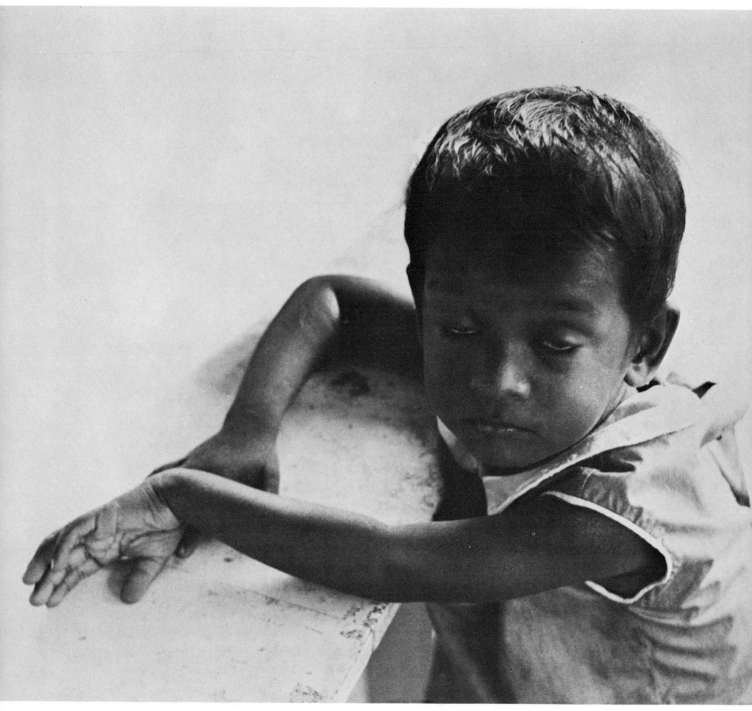

There are those who are not impressed by you and show it . . .

Even when mother does everything to make one smile sweetly.

Or a sister twists one's face to show its charm.

There is the expression of one who has eaten too much and is suffering.

There are gigglers. One who holds her nose . . .

And another who holds her mouth.

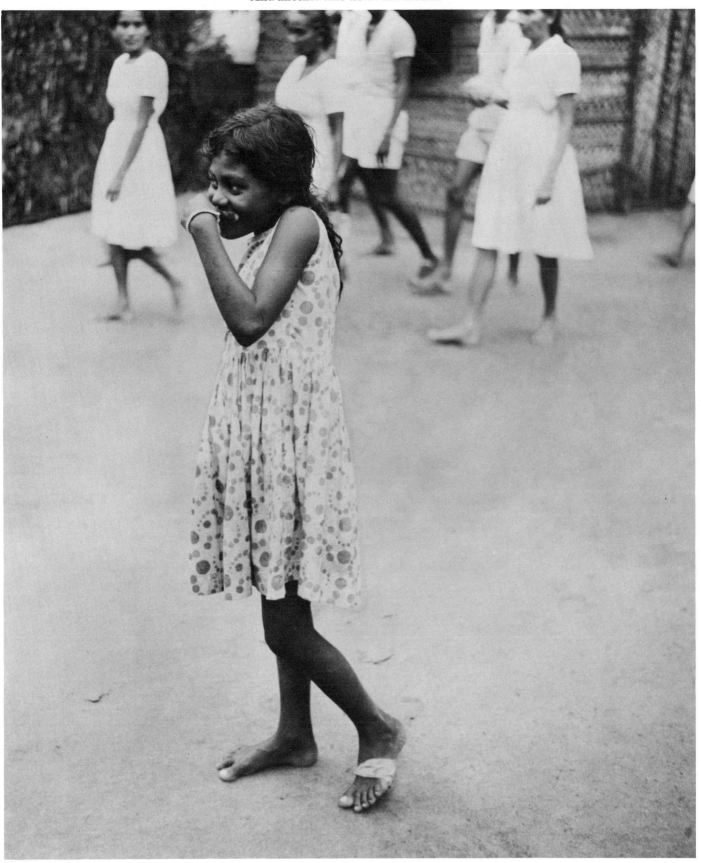

Then, there is the flirt.

A little girl who is a dreamer whether leaning on a wall . . .

Or twisting her hands in pleasant anticipation.

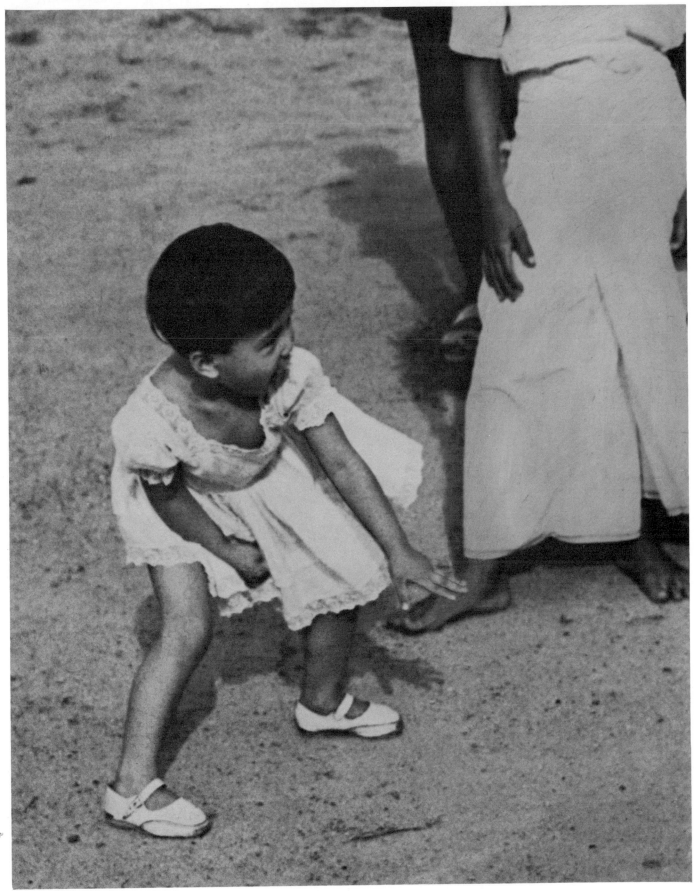

The audience participator who was more delightful to watch than the ball game she was watching.

This is not a picture of some goats. It is one of a boy who is goofing off by hiding above the goat pen. When he saw that I had seen him he was gone like a flash.

This is to me the story of the two sexes. The little boy studies the camera and a moment later could stand it no longer and came across to investigate. The little girl studies the little boy.

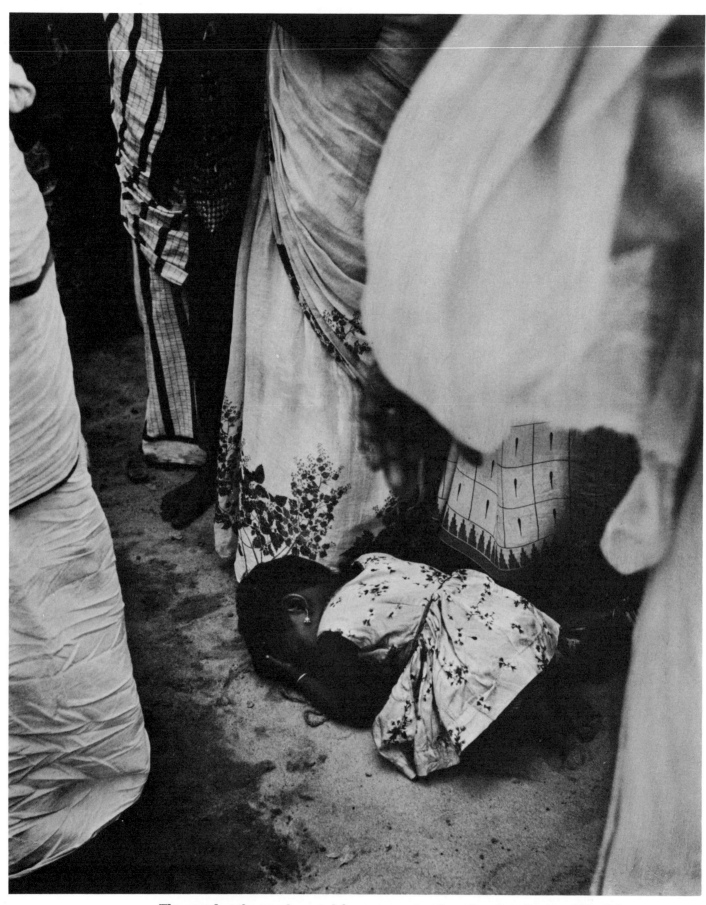

The crowd at the temple parted for a moment and on the ground was a little girl praying by herself.

9

When Father Steps In

Somehow it does not seem right to exclude fathers altogether. Particularly when, once in a while, they take the load off mother.

This father found himself with three daughters to dress after their bath in the river.
And he coped no more easily than a Western father in the same circumstances.

Father and son in Batticoloa market.

117

This is Guneya the most famous Kandyan dancer. His troupe include many youngsters who stand around him now while he dreses to dance in the Perehera. While
he fixes his anklet he balances easily on one foot.

10

The Older Generation

The older generation, the grandmothers, are some of the loveliest women in Ceylon. They look as grandmothers should look. Their hair is neither curled nor is it blue, and they are not tightly corseted so they can smile easily and often.

It is impossible not to love them.

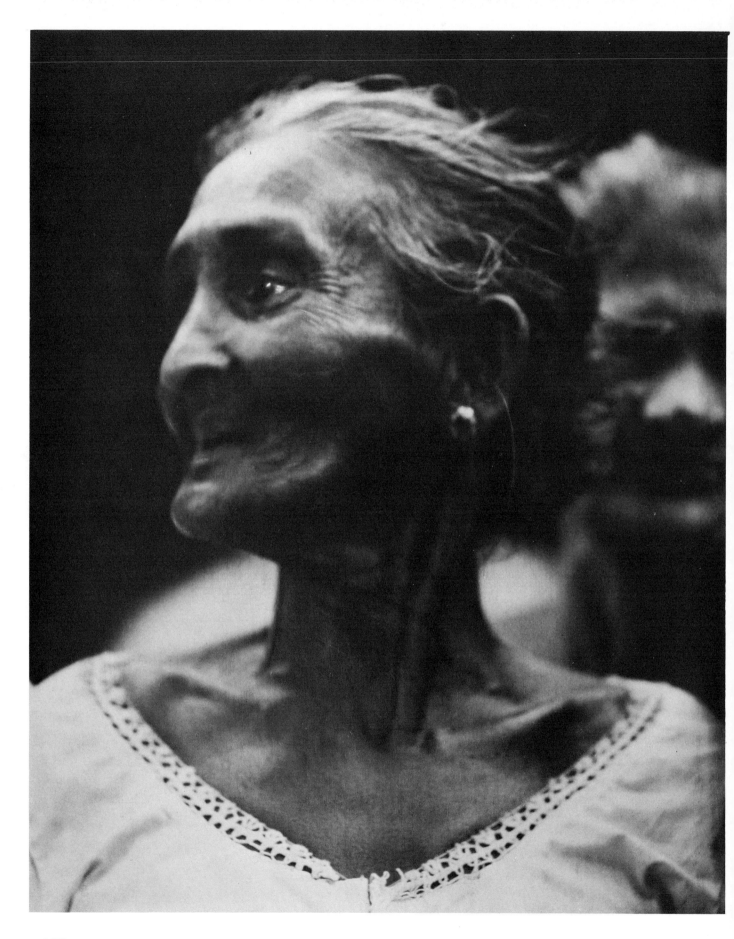

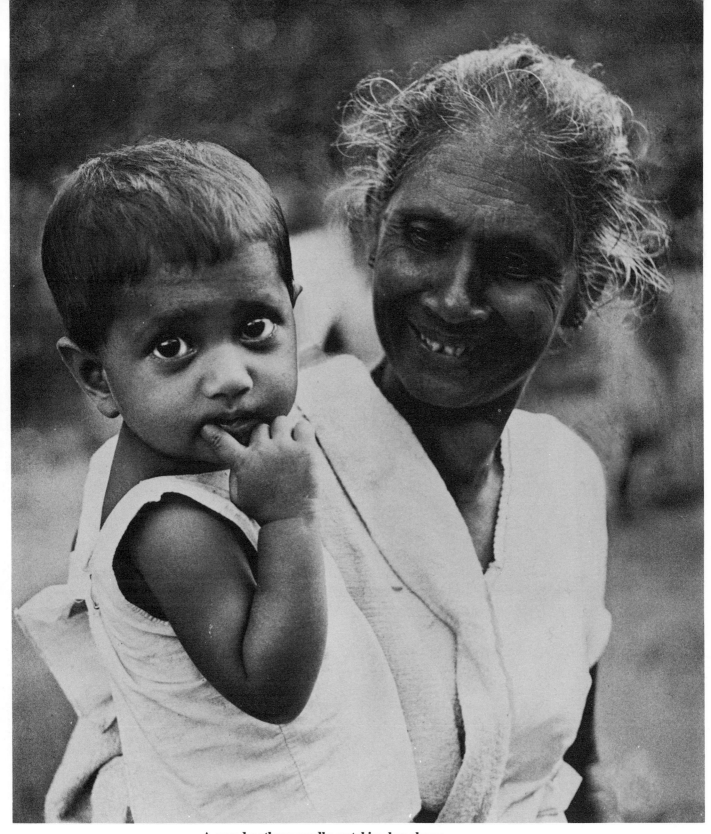

A grandmother proudly watching her charge.

A proud woman with a beautiful face.

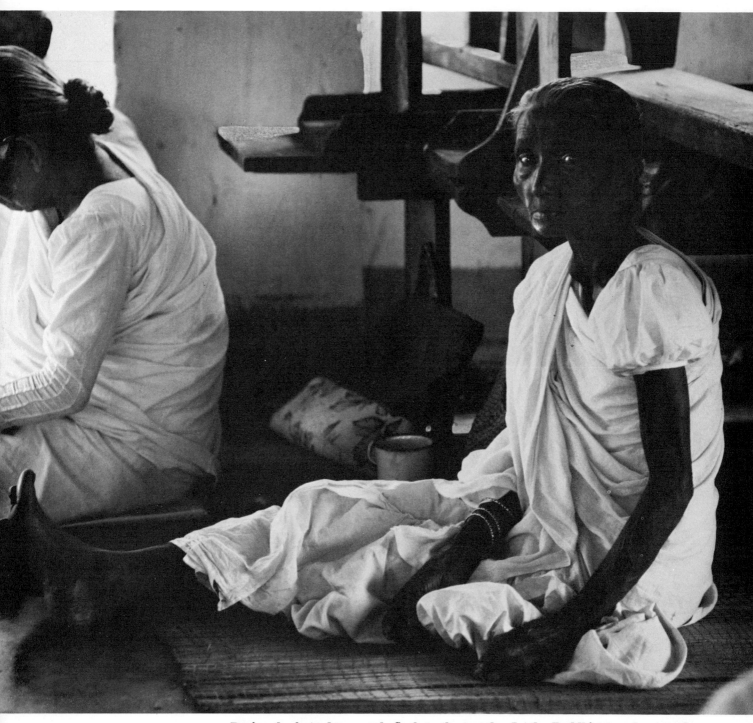

During the feast days people flock to the temple. In the Buddhist temple grounds there is an open room with low walls and pillars and a roof. Here many of the older people sit all day. They bring their food and rise from time to time to pray at the temple. These two women were among them.

Two faces from the market place in Colombo.

Two older women making their way along the street.

126

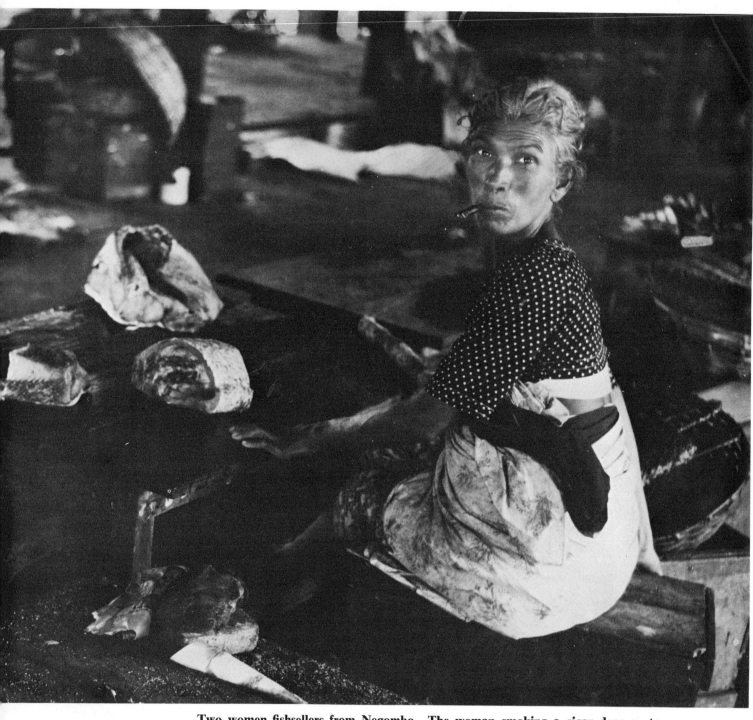

Two women fishsellers from Negombo. The woman smoking a cigar does so to kill the smell of the fish.

11

Miniature Mothers and Children

The little girls of Ceylon are miniature mothers, and their charges get the same loving care as they did. The older daughter of the family looks after the toddler as soon as she can carry him. The mother looks after the new baby. When they become teenagers, the daughters do all the household tasks as well.

This little girl proudly shows off her fat baby brother.

We walked down the beach between Negombo and Colombo followed by this little girl with her baby brother in her arms. Eventually he fell asleep but she continued to follow us. When we turned back she did too and she walked all the way back apparently untired. She smiled cheerfully most of the way, but by the time we got back my arms were aching in sympathy, while hers seemed as good as new.

Two little girls who are proud of their young charges.

Although the children were playing tag, the girl carrying the baby never once scowled or looked reluctantly at her heavy charge. She joined in as best she could, smiling all the time.